William the Conqueror and the Battle of Hastings

FRONT COVER: *An episode from the Bayeux Tapestry. The Anglo-Saxon infantry resists an attack by the Norman Cavalry on Battle hill.*

TOP: *An aerial view of Battle Abbey, founded by William the Conqueror on the battlefield of Hastings as a penance for the bloodshed.*

ABOVE: *The two lions of Normandy, emblem of a powerful state.*
BACK COVER: *The Great Gatehouse of Battle Abbey.*

William the Conqueror and the Battle of Hastings

R. Allen Brown, MA, DLitt, FSA,
Professor of History in the University of London King's College

Ten sixty-six is, by common consent, the most memorable date in English history. Everybody knows that the Battle of Hastings was fought in that year, and won by William the Conqueror of Normandy against Harold of England; also that this famous victory was decisive and represents the Norman Conquest of England. In remembering these things the popular instinct is sound, for it can and should be argued that the effects of the Conquest were cataclysmic. This, after all, is the Last Invasion. Nothing else remotely like it has happened since to cancel or alter its profound effects. Moreover the Normans, not content with England, went on to penetrate into Wales and Scotland (and ultimately into Ireland also) so that this is an affair of British and not

only English history. It is also an affair of European history, for it has been called 'England's first entry into Europe'. After 1066 and as the direct result of the Norman Conquest, England was integrated with northern France and became part of a continental political system in a way to which there is no earlier parallel save only the great but remote days of Roman Britain and the Roman Empire.

Much, we can see with hindsight, was thus at stake on Saturday, 14 October 1066, between 9 a.m. and dusk, at the place which has ever since been called Battle, but then was open country seven miles outside Hastings. ('King Harold . . . came against him at the hoary apple-tree', says the Anglo-Saxon Chronicle, as though there was no other landmark.) But how did the conflict come about?

The Norman Invasion in 1066 did not come out of the blue, nor was it simply a hostile invasion by a foreign foe, like that intended by Napoleon or Hitler. The historian must see it as the culmination of ever closer links with Normandy which began with the marriage in 1002 of Ethelred II (979-1016) to the Conqueror's ancestress Emma, daughter of the Norman duke, Richard I. William the Conqueror, son of Duke Robert the Magnificent born in 1027/8 at Falaise, certainly saw himself as the chosen heir of Edward the Confessor, himself the last Old English king and the son of Ethelred and the Norman Emma. There were other links too, more ethnic than political. The duchy of Normandy itself begins, in 911, as a Viking settlement in northern France, while half England had been settled by Vikings in Alfred's time and after, and the whole kingdom conquered by Cnut the Dane some fifty years before 1066.

According to what is sometimes called (by those loath to accept it)

the Norman version of events, King Edward (1042-66), who had spent most of his life to the age of almost 40 an honoured exile at the Norman court before his accession with Norman help in 1042, in 1051 nominated and caused to be formally 'recognised' as his heir by blood and choice the young Duke William. Edward had no heirs of his own by his wife Queen Edith, whom there is reason to suppose he disliked. She was the daughter of the dominant magnate, Godwin earl of Wessex, himself a creation of Cnut and the alleged murderer of Edward's brother, Alfred. Further, the Norman sources are unanimous that, at a date which must have been 1064, Edward the Confessor sent Earl Harold, the greatest magnate in his realm, to Normandy to confirm his earlier promise of the succession to Duke William. Harold, born c.1021/2 and by now himself Earl of Wessex, was the son of Godwin and his Danish wife, and this is the occasion of his famous oath, dramatically depicted as the centre-piece of the Bayeux Tapestry. According to the only detailed account of the event we have, by the contemporary William of Poitiers in his biography of the Norman duke, Harold did more than swear an oath to support William's succession: he became his feudal man, his vassal, by the solemn bonds of homage, fealty and investiture (by the last he was 'invested' with his lands and liberties in England, to be held as a fief of William as king).

When, therefore, Harold was crowned king on 6 January 1066, the very day of the deceased King Edward's funeral (and, according to the Norman sources, by Stigand, the uncanonically appointed archbishop of Canterbury and a creature of the house of Godwin), the two ceremonies following each other in the church of Westminster Abbey, the event in Norman eyes was not

only usurpation but felony and the sin of perjury.

As soon as the news reached Normandy, preparations were begun to vindicate Duke William's right, and those preparations included a kind of diplomatic offensive which won over most of the official public opinion of Europe to the Norman cause. Most important, the Papacy gave its blessing to the enterprise, that right might prevail and thereby also the English Church be reformed, which blessing was rather more than the equivalent of having the backing of the United Nations today. Against all this, it has to be noted that there is no 'English version of events' to set beside the Norman. The English sources are enigmatically and, as it may be thought, significantly silent on almost all the salient points in the Norman thesis (thus, as a striking example, no version of the Anglo-Saxon Chronicle has any entry for the crucial year 1064 at all), and Harold is not known to have made any diplomatic effort to justify his cause.

What, then, was Harold's cause? First, of course, on 6 January 1066 he became king *de facto*, which at this date means he was crowned and anointed king by the sacred rites of the Church – albeit probably at the hands of Stigand. Beyond that, he claimed to have received the dying bequest of the kingdom from King Edward on his death-bed – a factor which would certainly count for much if true. It was evidently accepted by the Normans, though in

★

FACING PAGE: *Early in the 11th century, King Cnut and Queen Emma place a gold cross on the high altar of the New Minster at Winchester.*

TOP: *Edward the Confessor, who founded Westminster Abbey, from a later manuscript.*

CENTRE: *Coin of Ethelred the Unready (above left); silver disc belonging to Emma (above right); coin depicting Cnut's profile (below left); silver penny of Edward the Confessor (below right).*

BELOW: *This family tree shows the close relationship between the ruling houses of England and Normandy.*

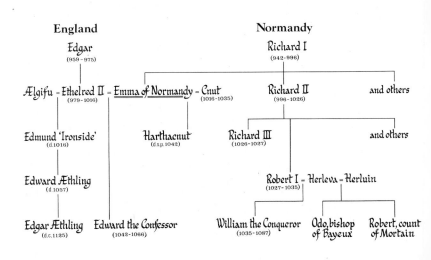

England

Edgar (959-975)

Ælgifu = Ethelred II = Emma of Normandy = Cnut (979-1016) (1016-1035)

Edmund 'Ironside' (d.1016)

Harthacnut (d.s.p.1042)

Edward Æthling (d.1057)

Edgar Æthling (d.c.1125)

Edward the Confessor (1042-1066)

Normandy

Richard I (942-996)

Richard II (996-1026)

and others

Richard III (1026-1027)

and others

Robert I = Herleva = Herluin (1027-1035)

William the Conqueror (1035-1087)

Odo, bishop of Bayeux

Robert, count of Mortain

their eyes made null and void by Harold's perjury and the earlier bequest to William with his recognition as King Edward's heir. Yet the one English contemporary source we have to describe the death-bed scene in detail makes the dying king say something rather different and rather less – 'I commend this woman [i.e. Edith, his wife and queen] and all the kingdom to your protection.' Harold also obtained recognition (which is the 'elective' element in early kingship) from the many magnates assembled in London for the Christmas feast and the dedication of the new church of Westminster which had taken place on 28 December, though since his coronation took place the day after the Confessor's death there was little time for consultation and none to consult those at a distance. There is evidence, indeed, that afterwards Harold had to win over the reluctant Northumbrians.

But if Harold could thus assemble in his favour a dying bequest by the reigning king, recognition by the magnates, and his actual coronation, the other and most vital element in the contemporary succession of kings was entirely lacking, namely kin right or blood right. Harold was, without question, the dominant figure in the court and kingdom of Edward the Confessor before 1066; his sister, Edith, was the queen; yet even so, he had no drop of royal blood. It is difficult therefore to see his succession as anything but a usurpation hastily disguised by legal forms and set in the context of political crisis. Certainly, in the words of the Anglo-Saxon Chronicle, 'he met little quiet in it as long as he ruled the realm'.

In the spring, Halley's comet appeared, to be taken by many as a sign and portent. 'Then over all England there was seen a sign in the skies such as had never been seen before. Some said it was the star "comet" which some call the long-haired star, and it first appeared on the Eve of the Greater Litany, that is 24 April, and so shone all the week' (the Chronicle again). In the late summer and autumn the Norman fleet and army assembled, first in mid-August, at Dives-sur-Mer near Caen, and then, from mid-September, at St-Valery-sur-Somme. The fleet was specially constructed for the purpose (as the Bayeux Tapestry vividly portrays), and the army reinforced by volunteers, from France and Picardy, from Brittany and Flanders.

But while William was waiting, and praying, for a favourable wind at St-Valery-sur-Somme, and after

*

Harold had been obliged, about 8 September, to dismiss his forces which all summer long had been guarding the south-east coast against the expected invasion ('The provisions of the people were gone, and nobody could keep them there any longer' – Anglo-Saxon Chronicle), England was invaded by a third force and third contender for the crown. This was Harold Hardrada, Harold the Ruthless, king of Norway, famous in saga and 'the last heroic figure of the Viking age'. He derived his claim from an alleged treaty of 1038-39 wherein his father, Magnus, and Harthacnut, the son of that Cnut who was king of Denmark, king of England and claimant to Norway, are said to have agreed that in the event of the death of either without heirs the other should succeed to the dominions of both. In 1042 Harthacnut did so die, and hence the claim of Magnus, and, after him, Harold Hardrada, to Denmark and to England.

In September 1066, Harold Hardrada took his chance and invaded England – and invaded in alliance with Tostig, Harold of England's own brother, former earl of Northumbria, deposed and banished in 1065, and now seeking his revenge. (These events may be thought a fitting commentary upon the sometimes exaggerated unity and strength of the pre-Conquest English kingdom.) The Norwegian force sailed up the Humber and the Ouse towards York, landed at Riccall, and defeated the northern earls Edwin and Morcar on Wednesday, 20 September, in a bloody engagement at Gate Fulford, then two miles from the city and now a suburb. York was entered in triumph and the citizens offered to join the victor (a further commentary) and march against the south – 'arranging that they should all go with him southwards and subdue this country' (Anglo-Saxon Chronicle).

At this point the scene is set for another great battle of 1066, which would be much better known had not Hastings cancelled its result three weeks later. As soon as he heard of the Norse invasion, Harold of England raised an army, and himself covered the near-200 miles from London by a forced march which brought him on 24 September to Tadcaster, where he marshalled and rested his troops for the night. On the morning of Monday, 25 September, he 'went right on through York' (Anglo-Saxon Chronicle) to fall upon the unprepared Norse by surprise at Stamford Bridge, seven miles on the other side of the city. Of the battle which followed we have little reliable information save that both sides fought it out on foot, in the ancient Teutonic and Viking manner, and that the result was devastating victory for the English king. Both Harold Hardrada and Tostig were slain, and the Norse army decimated. Some twenty ships, it is said, out of a reported invasion fleet of 300, sufficed to carry the survivors home.

Two days later, on 27 September, the Norman fleet sailed from the mouth of the Somme on the evening tide, having been granted at last a favourable wind after six weeks of difficult but disciplined waiting. They landed at Pevensey, unopposed, the next morning, raised a castle there within the Roman and Saxon fort of Anderida, and soon after moved on to a better base at Hastings where they raised another.

On or about 1 October, a week at most after his victory at Stamford Bridge, Harold received the news of their coming, traditionally at a celebratory feast at York. Again impressive speed is the keynote of

★

FACING PAGE: *Mont-St-Michel from the north-west, showing the original Norman part of the building.*

ABOVE RIGHT: *Part of the abbey of Jumièges still stands as a symbol of religious revival in Normandy in the 11th century.*

BELOW RIGHT: *A 17th-century engraving of the influential Benedictine abbey of Le Bec-Hellouin.*

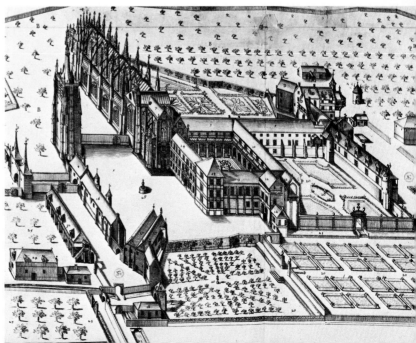

his action, but this time both precipitate and unwise. Within the space of thirteen days or less he had ridden again the 190 miles from York to London, assembled another army there, and accomplished a forced march of between fifty and sixty miles from London to what was to be the place of battle, where he arrived on the evening of Friday, 13 October.

Harold thus gave the Norman duke, with the minimum of delay, the decisive engagement which he wanted, and that, moreover, without obliging the Normans to leave their base and communications at Hastings to undertake the hazardous penetration of the interior of the kingdom. In so doing, the Eng-lish king also sacrificed numbers to speed, and all the English sources are agreed that the battle was joined 'before all the army had come' (Anglo-Saxon Chronicle). The object of it all was evidently what the Norman sources say, to take William by surprise – to repeat, in short, the tactics and the victory of Stamford Bridge.

William the Conqueror, however, now aged thirty-nine and with a long and brilliantly successful military career already behind him, in command of perhaps the finest fighting forces of the day, was not the man thus easily to be caught or out-manoeuvred. His scouts informed him of Harold's approach during the daylight hours of Friday.

That night, in anticipation of a possible night attack, the Normans stood to arms. At or before dawn (6.48a.m.) on Saturday 14 October, the Norman duke moved off in the known direction of the enemy, thus turning the tables, seizing the initiative, and in his turn, but in reality, taking Harold by surprise. From Telham Hill the English were observed, and the English scouts now also saw the Norman advance. The die was cast, and Harold, *faute de mieux*, drew up his ranks on the confined but otherwise good position of the ridge at Battle (according to Florence of Worcester, many deserted for lack of space), while William deployed his forces in the low ground to the south. At 9a.m., we are told by William of Poitiers, the battle began with 'the terrible sound of trumpets on both sides', to which cacophony the war cries of each side were soon to be added – *Deus aie*' ('God help us') from the Normans; 'Ut, ut' ('Out, out') and 'Ollie Crosse' (i.e. Harold's religious foundation of Waltham Holy Cross) from the English.

Because William the Conqueror founded Battle Abbey as penance, with the high altar of its church upon the spot where Harold fell, and because two major Norman sources, William of Poitiers and the incomparable Bayeux Tapestry, give detailed accounts of the battle (a third, 'The Song of the Battle of Hastings' is now thought to be later and unreliable, and the English sources are, as often, uncommunicative), we know probably more about Hastings than any other medieval battle. Some 7000 men on either side is the current estimate of the numbers involved, but for the Normans this includes some 2-3000 knights and their mounted esquires, while Harold's army all fought on

★

LEFT: *Harold may have prayed under this Anglo-Saxon chancel arch at Bosham before crossing the Channel to meet Duke William.*

FACING PAGE, ABOVE: *At Bayeux, Harold, touching a shrine and an altar, swears allegiance to William.*

FACING PAGE, BELOW: *The shrine in Westminster Abbey provided by Henry III in memory of Edward the Confessor.*

UBI HAROLD:SACRAMENTVM:FECIT:~ HIC HAROL
VVILLELMO DVCI:~

foot in the ancient manner, their élite force being the Anglo-Scandinavian housecarls, armed with their dreadful two-handed battle-axes, and then amongst the finest infantry in Europe.

Any army, its organization and its tactics, represents in all senses the society which forms it, and that the Old English fought on foot at Hastings demonstrates amongst other things that there the old world of Germanic and Carolingian society, reinforced by Vikings, faced and went down before the new and feudal world of Frankish chivalry. The tactics they adopted were time-honoured also, notably the very close formation picturesquely called the shield-wall, such as the ealdorman Brihtnoth had employed at Maldon over seventy years before. They were in such close order, wrote William of Poitiers, that the dead could scarcely fall. The housecarls were certainly massed in the centre about the king and his two brothers, Gyrth and Leofwine, and may also have composed or stiffened the entire front rank. The whole line, perhaps ten or twelve ranks in depth, extended some 600 or 800 yards along the ridge, i.e. 400 yards to the west of Harold's standard and headquarters (known from the position of the

9

DERVNT:HAROLDO: ÑA: REGIS hIC RE REX:AN SIDET:HAROLD GLORVM: STIGANT ARCHI EPS

high altar of Battle Abbey placed upon it) and 200 or 400 yards to the east (depending on whether the English left is put in the area of the present junction of the Hastings and Sedlescombe roads or in that of the present school). Their principal weapons were the spear and the sword in addition to the battle-axe, and there appears to have been a shortage of archers amongst them.

Against Harold, William deployed his army in three divisions, each of three orders. In the centre were the Normans with the duke himself, to the left (west) the Bretons and to the right (east) the 'French'. In the front of each division were placed the archers and (less certainly) crossbow-men: next came the heavy infantry; and behind them came the élite force of heavily armed and armoured mounted knights, the *force de frappe*, who, according to Anna Comnena writing some years later in far-off Constantinople, could pierce the walls of Babylon at the charge. The attack was launched by the Norman duke in that order, and the archers and infantry failing to make much impression, the Breton, French and Norman chivalry were soon in action, as they wished, hard-riding up the hill. 'Thus', wrote William of Poitiers, 'those who were last be-

came first.' The knights, indeed, though as a social no less than a military élite they have received most of the publicity and almost all the glamour ever since, did necessarily bear the brunt of the fighting on the Norman side that day, and in the end the victory was theirs. For the English, the last word and epilogue is best left to William of Malmesbury: 'They were few in number, but brave in the extreme.'

William of Poitiers, who had been a knight in the duke's service before he became a priest and ducal chaplain, observed with military perspicacity that this 'was a strange kind of battle, one side with all mobility and initiative, and the other just resisting as though rooted to the soil.' We, in our time, must not oversimplify. Hastings was a battle between infantry and cavalry, only in the sense that the English had no cavalry, not in the sense that the Normans had no infantry. Also it was a long and hard engagement, the issue not decided until dusk and the death of the king, the shock tactics and the *élan* of the knightly contingents very nearly cancelled out by the English defensive position on the crest of the ridge.

Although the principal Norman sources between them make entirely clear the opening phases of the

battle, they could not or did not keep up a blow-by-blow account of so long an engagement, and something of the fog of war settled upon their narratives if not upon participants. Two outstanding incidents in the course of the long day are clear, however: namely the near-disaster of an incipient retreat by the Norman forces, and the tactic of the feigned flight employed by the Norman knights.

The first, because Hastings and the Norman Conquest are still controversial and arouse strong feelings now as well as then, is seized on with relish by would-be English-sympathizers and at times is almost turned into an English victory. At some point the Bretons on the Norman left began to give way. The movement spread and was made worse by a flying rumour that the duke himself was dead. This alone, according to William of Poitiers, made even the Normans fall back. Then some of the English, with or without orders, advanced down the hill in pursuit. The rot was stopped by the intrepid duke, with the help of some of his closest companions. Spurring his horse in front of those who were fleeing, he bared his head to show his face, shouting 'Look at me. I am alive and with God's help shall be the victor! What madness

10

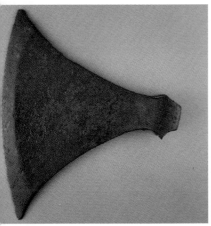

TOP: *Claiming a death-bed bequest of the kingdom by Edward, Harold is crowned King. Some acclaim him, others fear the comet as foretelling doom. Ghost ships of the coming Norman invasion appear in the lower border.*

ABOVE: *An axe-head found in London, typical of the two-handed Anglo-Saxon battle-axe wielded by Harold's infantry.*

RIGHT: *A page from the Anglo-Saxon Chronicle, 'E', for the years 1066–8.*

11

ABOVE: *Coats of mail, helmets, lances and swords, together with barrels of wine, are carried to William's ships. Norman horsemen wore mail in battle, whereas the foot soldiers were often less well protected. The hauberk, or mail shirt, was knee-length, had three-quarter length sleeves and was split from hem to fork to allow freedom of movement on horseback. It was often constructed of interlinked, riveted rings, forming a very strong, pliable armour.*

LEFT: *This 12th-century Bible illustration, depicting Goliath, gives a clear impression of a fighting foot-soldier. He holds his spear above his head to attack with a downward stabbing movement. Such a hold would also enable the soldier to throw the spear if necessary. His large shield is held in his left hand by straps attached to the inside. The shield is long, giving protection to most of his body; the pointed shape allows it to be used on horseback also.*

FACING PAGE, ABOVE: *Grouped around Duke William's vessel, the Norman fleet, complete with horses, approaches Pevensey. The ships are Viking in style.*

FACING PAGE, BELOW: *Pevensey Castle, East Sussex.*

ET VENIT AD PEVENESÆ :-

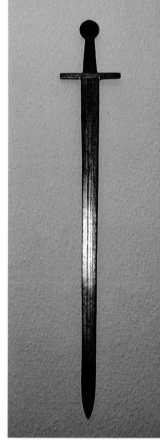

leads you to flight?' The scene is vividly depicted on the Tapestry, where William raises his helmet, Count Eustace of Boulogne points to him, and Odo, bishop of Bayeux and the Conqueror's half-brother, brandishing his mace, encourages and turns back 'the boys', the young men and esquires who are seeking to quit this terrifying first blooding. Thereafter, we are told, the Conqueror himself led a counter-charge, sword in hand, and those of the English who had broken ranks in pursuit were cut down and destroyed.

The stratagem of the feigned flight, according to William of Poitiers (whose account is to be preferred), was employed after the real retreat. It has been denied, in the teeth of all the evidence, by most modern military historians on no other ground than their own ill-informed conviction that medieval warfare in general, and 'feudal' warfare in particular, was undisciplined, and therefore no such disciplined manoeuvre could possibly have taken place. In reality, there is no reason whatsoever why these

professional warriors and superb horsemen, trained from their early youth up to fight on horseback and to do so together in their contingents or *conrois*, should not have used this well-tried tactic. All the written accounts of Hastings tell us they did, and, as we know from other and independent sources, Norman knights of this generation also used it at St Aubin-le-Cauf near Arques in 1052-53 and near Messina in 1060. The object, successfully accomplished, was to lure down parties of the English from their ranks upon the ridge and then, wheeling about, to cut them down piecemeal while the main position was thus weakened.

Yet still the main position held, though the Normans and their allies continued their unrelenting pressure. They shot arrows, cut with their swords, thrust with their lances, wrote William of Poitiers, and in his Latin one can almost hear the percussion – '*Sagittant, feriunt, perfodiunt Normanni.*' Only as daylight faded (*'Iam inclinato die . . .'*), and King Harold himself, his brothers, Gyrth and Leofwine, long

since slain, fell at the foot of his standard, did the remnants of the Old English army break and leave the field, ruthlessly pursued and ridden down by the Norman knights, hot in the fire of victory. Darkness had descended before the victorious Norman duke, involved in this as in all things, the stump of a broken lance in his hand, rode back on to the battlefield, now covered

★

ABOVE LEFT: *William has a castle built at Hastings, to provide a strong-point. The motte, or mound of earth, would be encircled by a ditch and surmounted by a palisade and timber tower.*

ABOVE RIGHT: *A beautifully preserved sword dating from between 1050 and 1125.*

FACING PAGE, ABOVE: *Battle Abbey overlooks the battlefield. Marshes at the foot of the hill were an additional hazard for William's men.*

FACING PAGE, BELOW: *Carefully drawn by General E. Renouard James, this plan shows the probable deployment of the two armies.*

far and wide with the slain nobility and youth of England.

There followed, the next day, the burial of Harold, under an inscribed stone on the shore near Hastings, by William Malet by order of the Conqueror, and then the slow, circuitous, intimidating advance upon Winchester and London, crossing the Thames at Wallingford, planting castles and receiving submissions along the way. London was eventually entered towards midwinter, evidently without opposition, and, while castles were raised there also (one of them the future Tower of London) 'against the inconstancy of the huge and brutal populace' (William of Poitiers), preparations were put in hand for the Conqueror's coronation. It took place on Christmas Day, 1066, in the great new church of Westminster (built prophetically by Edward the Confessor on the model of Jumièges and the great churches then rising in Normandy), which had now been the scene, in this its memorable first year, of one royal funeral and two crownings.

There is much more to military history than battles, even decisive

ones like Hastings, and it must certainly be asked how on earth it came about that Normandy, scarcely larger than the single English province of East Anglia, could thus defeat and conquer the far larger and potentially stronger ancient English kingdom. Antiquity and its reverse, indeed, have much to do with it, for everything in mid-11th-century Normandy was new, and the Norman state (for such it was) at the apex of a period of what modern jargon would call growth, expanding, prosperous, rich and, above all, self-confident. Norman society was of that new and ebullient type, then prevalent in northern France especially, which we call feudal. 'Society organized for war', the text-books rightly say, but more than this, one dominated by a professional warrior élite of knights, lords of the land as of the battlefield, excelling in the art of a new type of warfare which exploited above all the shock tactics of heavy cavalry and the fortified base of the castle, bound together by the ties of vassalage culminating in the prince above them. Norman society was also essentially aristocratic, its

origins the Viking warriors first established in and about Rouen in 911. Thereafter they created the duchy of Normandy, imposing themselves upon a countryside deserted by its former lords and clergy, in the process adopting and developing Frankish religion and culture as well as warfare, Frankish laws and customs, and surviving notions of Carolingian government. It was also expansionist, and in the course of the 11th century broke out of the confines of Normandy to take over all Southern Italy and Sicily – an amazing achievement by freelance knights and companies of knights even more impressive in its way than the conquest of England. Against all this the more ancient Old English kingdom, politically and even ethnically divided, its society as yet untouched by feudal concepts, its military system and Teutonic tactics in consequence alike out of date, and in any case commanded by Harold's over-confident and faulty generalship, could not prevail, nor in the end indefinitely resist.

In any explanation of Norman victory in England, William the Conqueror himself must have high place. He was a very perfect Christian prince. He not only presided over Norman society at the apogee of its power and *élan* but directed and inspired it, and harnessed its resources to his will. He could manage men. He had a near-perfect marriage to a near-perfect wife. As a ruler he kept firm peace and did good justice. He was not only the happy warrior who in 1066 had never lost a battle nor failed to take a castle, he was also the pious head of his Norman church, the friend and patron especially of monks. Beyond doubt William believed in the justice of his cause, and saw Hastings as the Judgement of God against the perjured Harold.

Whatever else the Normans were, excelling in monasticism no less than war, they were not philistines, as even to us their art and architecture demonstrate. They were not motivated solely by the cult of violence and the lust for gain. Although we may live in an allegedly secular society we shall never understand the past without religion. Normandy in the mid-11th century

ET FRANCI INPRELIO

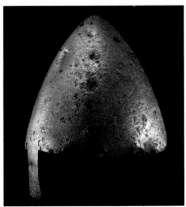

FACING PAGE: *11th-century infantry and cavalry, in this case wearing no armour, but relying on helmets and shields for protection.*

TOP: *A moment of triumph for some of Harold's men as they successfully hold a hillock, while Norman knights are swallowed up in the marshes.*

ABOVE: *Conical in shape, this Norman helmet has a strip of steel to protect the nose and face.*

RIGHT: *Harold's housecarls form a shield wall to give secure defence against cavalry attack.*

17

was at the high point of a great religious revival, led by the duke himself. All over the duchy great churches, cathedral and monastic, were rising to make this manifest, as many of them still survive to do – Jumièges, Mont-St-Michel, Caen (St Stephen's and Holy Trinity), Cerisy-la-Forêt and Lessay – and as many more still bigger were to rise in England after 1066 – St Albans and Winchester, Norwich and Chichester, Gloucester and Durham and others. The Norman Church, ruled over by the same families who ruled the duchy, and firmly under the direction of the duke, did as much to unify and to integrate Normandy as ducal government or the ties of vassalage, and contributed even more to that conscious sense of *Normanitas* which carried all before it in the 11th century, in England, in southern Italy and Sicily, and in Antioch on the First Crusade. Yet this is no mere exercise of muscular Christianity in 11th-century form. The Norman Church was in the van of a general ecclesiastical reform movement then developing in Latin Christendom and increasingly centred upon Rome, its monasteries

especially outstanding, the monastic schools – Fécamp, St Evroult, Bec above all – amongst the most distinguished for their scholarship in Europe. Nowhere were things spiritual and material, God and Caesar, separated, whether in the duke's government, the ceremonies of vassalage, or on the battlefield. Duke William invaded England in 1066 in a just war with the blessing of the Papacy, the highest moral authority in Europe, to vindicate his right, the whole enterprise set in the context of a developing notion of Holy War which in the next generation would bring forth the Crusade.

The Norman Conquest was William's particular achievement, and thereafter as 'William the Great' and king of the English he was one of the greatest of England's kings. He is thus ultimately responsible for the profound changes which that Conquest brought about. As the result of 1066 English history was set upon a new course and no event since has done more to produce modern England and modern Britain. First, the ruling dynasty was changed in an age when monarchy was personal as well as power-

ful. Second, the entire ruling class was changed, in church as well as state, and this in an age when a ruling class really ruled. England was under new management after Hastings, and nothing could ever be the same again, nor was it. In fact, the whole nature of society was changed, from an ancient Germanic and Carolingian type of social organization, still surviving in pre-Conquest England and merely reinforced by Viking settlement, to a feudal organization now naturally and unconsciously brought in by the new lords of the land from Normandy and northern France. And this in turn involves so many lasting changes that it is almost impossible to list them in any short account.

Feudalism, thus, greatly increased the power of the king, now feudal suzerain as well as monarch, and bound society, through vassalage and tenure, much more closely than had been the case before. Rapidly growing royal power, which forms the sinews of the state, and a new degree of political unity, are not the least important results of Hastings. The

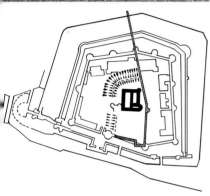

ENTRY TO THE TRAITORS GATE

FACING PAGE: *It is probable that Harold was first struck by an arrow in his right eye, but that his death-blow came from the sword of a Norman knight.*

TOP: *A French inscription commemorates Harold's death on this memorial at Battle Abbey.*

ABOVE RIGHT: *The Tower of London, i.e. the royal castle of London, was founded by the Conqueror in 1066 in the south-east corner of the city, to overawe the Londoners and defend the eastern approaches by land and water. The great White Tower, i.e. 'The Tower', was built within the castle soon afterwards, contained the king's accommodation and was the symbol of his regality.*

ABOVE: *Ground plan of the Tower of London showing in darker outline the original castle of the Conquest, the White Tower, and the Roman city wall, all within the great extensions and developments of the twelfth and thirteenth centuries.*

RIGHT: *Norman chapel of St John the Evangelist in the White Tower.*

19

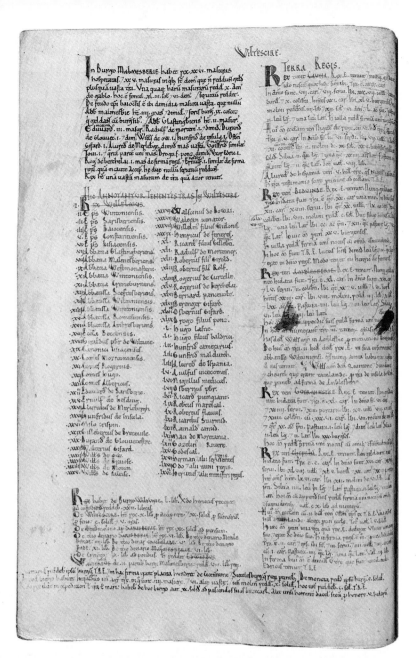

Old English monarchy, created by Alfred and his successors, was the kingdom of Wessex writ large, essentially southern, and should probably be seen, in modern terms, as more federal than national – Wessex, Mercia, Northumbria and the Danelaw. Edward the Confessor, for example, had never been north of the Humber on the day he died. William the Conqueror by contrast was in the north, for the second time, in the grim winter of 1069-70, and crushed it, by that 'Devastation of the North' which has been condemned by his critics then and since but which was a crucial event in the history of England. The Normans also went on to penetrate deep into Wales, into southern Scotland, and ultimately into Ireland.

Meanwhile the Domesday Survey of 1086, unique as an administrative achievement until the 19th century, its contents painstakingly arranged in terms of feudal tenure (who holds what, and of whom), is as great a monument to Norman governmental efficiency as their buildings are to Norman wealth and power and to Norman artistic and technological skills. Their buildings, castles and churches alike, point to another sociological change which Domesday Book records: a far greater concentration of wealth in the hands of far fewer than had prevailed before.

Feudalism and the Conquest also combined to bring about a great expansion in royal justice, and accelerated those processes which were soon to produce the English Common Law – and how, one may ask, can political unity be brought about without a common law? Feudalism, moreover, profoundly altered the substance of English law, for feudalism involves a new form of tenure and in this age and for long

after, the land law was nine-tenths of the law of the land. Feudalism, too, most obviously involves a new form of military organization and a new type of warfare, based on the knight and the castle. The two or three things that every schoolboy really does still know about the medieval and feudal periods are knights and chivalry and castles, and all of them begin in England in 1066. And though the knights and even the chivalry are now gone, the hundreds of castles that remain throughout the length and breadth of the land, from Newcastle to Dover and from Pembroke to Norwich, mark to this day the pace and permanence of the Norman settlement and the new social order of feudal lordship. The men of England's new feudal aristocracy, from the king downwards, were born and bred to war – born, we may say, in the castle and brought up in the saddle – and as Normans and Anglo-Normans they waged it increasingly in France. If war is the catalyst of change, which it is, and if one is interested in the history of modern Europe as well as England, then war between England and France, which begins after 1066 and continues to 1815 and beyond, must come high on any list of the most important results of the Conquest.

The Church was scarcely less affected than the state and secular society, nor could it be otherwise when the same ruling families dominated all three no less than in Jane Austen's England. The Church, indeed, was feudalized, as

★

FACING PAGE, ABOVE: *A page from the Domesday Book of 1086.*

FACING PAGE, BELOW LEFT: *Charter of William I confirming the rights exercised by London's citizens under Edward the Confessor.*

FACING PAGE, BELOW RIGHT: *Penny of William the Conqueror.*

ABOVE RIGHT: *Magnificent Norman arches with painted decoration, built by Abbot Paul of Caen, at St Albans.*

RIGHT: *'Abraham brings back Lot' from a book of philosophy executed c.1100 at St Albans. Biblical figures are depicted as Normans and English.*

most bishops and many abbots were required to send knights to the king's service in return for their lands, which were now held in part as fiefs. But of course this was not all, and the Normans brought reform with them from Normandy and the Continent. Under the Conqueror and Lanfranc his archbishop – who, like many of the new Norman prelates now taking over the English Church, came from Bec – English monasticism was revived, altered and greatly extended (in the north now as well as the south), and the whole church reorganized and therewith reinvigorated. The Anglo-Norman Church, however, with its own synods and councils, courts and jurisdiction, more autonomous than its Old English predecessor, was no less firmly under royal control, and neither William nor Lanfranc approved the new papal claims at this time to government of a universal Church from Rome. And over all, symbolizing both a new spirit and a new lordship, rose the great new Norman churches, many still standing, far bigger, and surely better, than anything that had gone before. Every major church in England was rebuilt in the new style of Norman Romanesque within a generation or two of Hastings save only Westminster, already built by Edward the Confessor on the Norman model, and Harold's Waltham Holy Cross which now could obviously find no patron. 'After their [the Normans'] coming to England', wrote William of Malmesbury, 'they revived the rule of religion which had there grown lifeless. You might see great churches rise in every village, and, in the towns and cities, monasteries built after a style unknown before.'

With ecclesiastical architecture especially goes art, and with the

*

WINCHESTER
THE OLD AND NEW MINSTERS

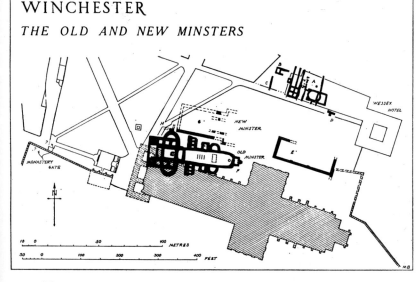

TOP: *William I as church-builder, from a later manuscript.*
ABOVE: *Effigy of Bishop Herbert de Losinga at Norwich, c.1100.*
ABOVE RIGHT: *The abbey church of St Stephen founded by William at Caen.*
RIGHT: *Tomb of William the Conqueror in the choir of St Stephen's.*

23

Church goes learning. While many maintain (though not all agree) that while the Normans excelled in the major art of architecture the Old English had excelled in some or all of the lesser arts of sculpture, painting, metalwork and embroidery, there can be no doubt that the Conquest marks a reception in England of the new Norman and French Latin learning in place of the Old English vernacular culture, old-fashioned and inward-looking. This alone 'made of England a province of the commonwealth of Latin Europe' (David Knowles). And here we reach the most profoundly important change of all wrought by the Norman Conquest. By kings and lords and the ramifications of family relationships, by tenure and vassalage, by social organization, custom and outlook, by ecclesiastical reform, learning and culture, and also by the waging of

war, England was turned from a largely barren pre-Conquest affiliation with Scandinavia, and integrated with northern France, the central force of medieval, and thus European, civilization. It would be difficult to wish it had been otherwise. The historical world is still surprisingly divided into Anglo-Saxons and Normans, and the last argument of the former is that all this would, might or could have happened anyway by some other means. But the inescapable fact is that it happened in 1066 as the direct result of the Battle of Hastings, and one may still end any account of the Norman Conquest of England with Carlyle's splendid rhetorical question – 'Without them [the Normans']... what had it ever been?' One may add to it that without the Conqueror himself, who died on 9 September 1087, none of it would have happened.

ABOVE: *Effigy of Robert, Duke of Normandy, eldest son of William I, at Gloucester.*

ACKNOWLEDGEMENTS

Pictures of the Bayeux Tapestry on the front cover and pp. 9 top, 10, 11 top, 12 top, 13 top, 14 left, 17 top, 17 bottom right, 18, are reproduced with the special permission of the Ville de Bayeux.

Other pictures are acknowledged as follows: Aerofilms: pp. 1 top, 13 bottom; Bodleian Library: pp. 1 bottom, 11 bottom right; British Library: pp. 2, 3 top, 21 bottom, 23 top left; Ashmolean Museum: p. 3 centre (top and bottom left); British Museum: pp. 3 centre (top and bottom right), 11 bottom left, 20 bottom right; Robert Clarke Studio: inside cover, p. 3 bottom: The Pierpoint Morgan Library: p. 4; Sonia Halliday and Laura Lushington: p. 5 top; Yves le Clerc: p. 23 bottom right; Zodiaque: pp. 6, 7 top, 23 top right; Burgerbibliothek, Bern: p. 5 bottom; Bibliothèque Nationale: pp. 7 bottom, 16; Duncan McNeill: p. 8; Gerald Newbery: pp. 9 bottom, 19 bottom right, 21 top, 24; Bibliothèque Publique de Dijon: p. 12 bottom; Ian Peirce: pp. 14 right, 15 top; Society of Antiquaries of London: pp. 15 bottom (from *Domesday Tables* by Francis Baring, 1909), 22 bottom (Winchester Excavations Committee); Kunsthistorisches Museum, Vienna: p. 17 bottom left; Ronald Sheridan: p. 19 top left; Angelo Hornak: pp. 19 top right, 22 top; Public Record Office: p. 20 left; The Corporation of London Records Office: p. 20 bottom left; Jarrold, Norwich: p. 23 bottom left; Crown Copyright, Department of the Environment Photographic Library: back cover.

ISBN 0 85372 442 3